# Sea Turtles

## Judy Wearing

Published by Weigl Publishers Inc.
350 5th Avenue, 59th Floor
New York, NY 10118
Website: www.weigl.com

Library of Congress Cataloging-in-Publication Data

Wearing, Judy.
 Sea turtle / Judy Wearing.
    p. cm. --  (World of wonder)
 Includes index.
 ISBN 978-1-60596-106-4 (hard cover : alk. paper) -- ISBN 978-1-60596-107-1 (soft cover : alk. paper)
 1.  Sea turtles--Juvenile literature.  I. Title.
 QL666.C536W427 2010
 597.92'8--dc22

                          2009004987


Printed in the United States in North Mankato, Minnesota
2 3 4 5 6 7 8 9 0  13 12 11 10

042010
WEP060410

Editor: Heather C. Hudak
Design and Layout: Terry Paulhus

All of the Internet URLs given in the book were valid at the time of publication. However, due to the dynamic nature of
the Internet, some addresses may have changed, or sites may have ceased to exist since publication. While the author
and publisher regret any inconvenience this may cause readers, no responsibility for any such changes can be accepted
by either the author or the publisher.

Weigl acknowledges Getty Images as its primary image supplier for this title.

# CONTENTS

# What is a Sea Turtle?

Have you ever seen an animal that looks like a giant seashell with legs and a head swimming in the water? This may have been a sea turtle. Sea turtles are **reptiles**, just like snakes and lizards. They live in the ocean, but they still need to breathe air.

Some sea turtles can stay underwater for more than two hours when they are resting. Most people can hold their breath for less than one minute.

# Turtle Types

Did you know that some sea turtles are bigger than humans? Leatherback turtles grow to 8 feet (2.4 meters) long. They weigh about 1,500 pounds (700 kilograms). The smallest type of sea turtle is the Kemp's ridley turtle. It grows to 30 inches (76 centimeters).

There are five other types of sea turtles. These are the flatback, green, loggerhead, olive ridley, and hawksbill. Most of these turtles are 2 to 4 feet (0.6 to 1.2 m) long.

# Shell Shock

What do sea turtles have in common with humans? They have a hard shell that is made from the same **substance** as human bones. The parts of the shell fit together like puzzle pieces. The shell is covered with scales. It protects the turtle's body.

The leatherback turtle's shell is special. It is leathery and oily, with many small bones inside.

Even sharks cannot bite through a sea turtle's hard shell.

# Sea Snacks

What do sea turtles like to eat? Different kinds of sea turtles eat different foods.

The green turtle eats plants that grow close to shore. This is where the green turtle spends most of its time. The hawksbill turtle uses its sharp **beak** to find small plants and animals in rocks and **coral**.

Leatherback turtles eat jellyfish that they catch in the deep, open ocean. These turtles have **spines** in their throats that help them swallow their slippery meal.

# Long Way Home

Did you know that sea turtles go back to the same beach where they were born to lay their eggs? Sometimes, this **journey** is thousands of miles. Scientists think turtles have a kind of **compass** in their brains to help them find their way.

The only time sea turtles go on land is when they lay eggs. Female turtles lay eggs every two to three years.

# Beach Babies

How many eggs do sea turtles lay? They lay more than 100 round, rubbery eggs at once.

On summer nights, female sea turtles climb onto a beach. There, they dig deep holes in the sand. They lay eggs in only one hole. Then, they cover the eggs with sand to hide them from **predators**. The turtles go back into the water and do not visit the nest again. In two months, the baby turtles begin to hatch.

If the sand is very hot after the eggs are laid, more females will be born. More males are born if the sand is very cold.

# Which Way is the Ocean?

How do sea baby turtles find the water? When the turtles hatch, they look for light and follow it to the water.

Baby turtles leave their nest at night. The Moon over the ocean makes the water shiny and bright. The turtles move toward the light to find the water.

Birds, raccoons, and crabs wait on the beach to eat baby turtles. More animals wait in the ocean. Only a few baby turtles will live to be adults.

# Flipper Feet

How do sea turtles swim? Unlike land turtles, sea turtles do not have legs. Instead, they have large, flat **flippers** that look like ping pong paddles. These flippers help push sea turtles through water quickly. Some sea turtles can swim at speeds up to 20 miles (32 kilometers) per hour.

# Turtles of Tomorrow

What dangers do sea turtles face? Most kinds of sea turtles are endangered. This means there are not many left. Some sea turtles get caught in fishing nets and cannot breathe. Others eat plastic bags or balloons that humans toss into the water where turtles live. Finding better ways to fish or throwing away garbage properly can help sea turtles.

Some of the places where sea turtles live are being destroyed to build human homes. Baby turtles walk toward light from houses instead of the light over the water. They never reach the sea.

# Hide the Nest

**Supplies**
a large sheet of yellow construction paper, a pencil, scissors, tape

1. Turtles sometimes dig many nests in the sand. They cover them all up, even though they only put eggs in one of them. They do this to hide the real nest. On a sheet of paper, draw a turtle nest with eggs inside.

2. Turn over the sheet of paper, and put a small "x" on the back where your nest is.

3. Bury the nest with sand by cutting out a piece of construction paper and taping it over top.

4. Draw other nests on the sheet of paper, but do not show any eggs inside.

5. Bury your fake nests by by cutting out a piece of construction paper and taping it over top.

6. Ask a friend to try to find the real nest.

7. You can try this with real sand by digging nests in a sandbox and using ping pong balls as eggs.

# Find Out More

To learn more about sea turtles, visit these websites.

**Caribbean Conservation Corporation & Sea Turtle Survival League**
www.cccturtle.org/
turtletides.php

**Sea Turtle Rescue and Rehabilitation Center**
www.seaturtlehospital.org

**SeaWorld**
www.seaworld.org/infobooks/
SeaTurtle/home.html

**National Geographic Kids**
www.nationalgeographic.com/
ngkids/9911/turtle/index.html

# Glossary

**beak:** a hard mouth structure that sticks out

**compass:** a tool that uses a magnet to tell direction

**coral:** a hard, stony substance that is made by a soft animal living in the ocean

**flippers:** wide, flat limbs used for swimming

**journey:** a long trip

**predators:** animals that hunt other animals for food

**reptiles:** cold-blooded animals that are covered in scales and lay soft-shelled eggs on land

**spines:** thin, stiff, pointy parts of the body

**substance:** a type of matter

# Index